Contents

What is a farm?

A farm is a place where food is grown.

Farmers use many different machines.

Tractors

A tractor is a farm machine.

Tractors can pull other machines.

Planting

A plough is a farm machine.

A plough digs up the ground for planting.

A plough can be pulled by oxen.

This farm machine spreads manure to help plants grow.

Growing plants

This machine plants seeds.

The seeds grow into plants.

This machine waters the plants.

This machine kills harmful insects.

Picking plants

The plants are ready to pick.

This machine cuts wheat.

This machine picks grapes.

This machine packs straw.

Caring for farm machines

Farm machines are very important.

Farmers must take good care of their machines.

Can you remember?

What does a plough do?

Answer on page 24

Picture glossary

manure most manure is made from animal poo. It can help plants to grow.

oxen cows or bulls that are trained to pull ploughs or do other farm jobs

plough farm machine that breaks up the ground so that farmers can plant seeds

seed plants grow from seeds. Farmers plant seeds in the ground.

Index

Answer to quiz on page 22: A plough digs up the ground to get it ready for planting.

Notes to parents and teachers

Before reading

Ask the children if they have ever visited a farm. Ask them what machines they might find on a farm. Make a list together and see if they know what each machine is used for. Why do they think farmers need machines?

After reading

- Put the children into groups and give them a range of modelling materials. Ask them to make a model of a tractor or other farm machine from the book. Make sure they have plenty of circular plastic or card to make wheels. When the models are ready the children can paint them and make a farm display.
- Sing "This is the way…" building in words about farm machines. For example: "This is the way we plough the field, plough the field, plough the field, This is the way we plough the field, Early in the morning." Other verses could include: This is the way we pull the trailer, This is the way we plant the seeds, This is the way we cut the wheat, etc. You could hold up pictures of each machine to prompt the children once they have learned the song.